JUMPSTART
dive into Jesus. transform the world.

BRIAN ORME

JUMPSTART

Jumpstart is a simple manual to help you dive into Jesus and transform the world. It's a powerful means to assist you in understanding all that Jesus has done and who you are in Him. Jesus didn't just give us a set of teachings; He gave us Himself. He is the Truth. As you dive into this tool, the hope is that you will uncover all that God has done for you, experience His unrelenting love, and become more and more confident as a son/daughter in His Kingdom. Take a deep breath, open wide your eyes and ears, and take the plunge into the most incredible journey of your life.

© Copyright 2013 Brian Orme
www.kingdomstrate.com
ISBN-13: 9780615866116
ISBN-10: 0615866115
Editors: Elizabeth Chung, Katy Brelje, and Emmanuel Pun
Design: Brian Orme and Raechel Wong

TABLE OF CONTENTS

PHASE I — WHAT JUST HAPPENED?

Welcome to your spiritual family! You have just made the most life-altering decision you will ever make: to follow Jesus, and we want to celebrate it with you. Below, you will find several helpful biblical scriptures, along with a few questions that will hopefully bring insight to all that has happened and is happening. Let's get started with all the good things that have taken place.

> Romans 10:9-10 (NLT) — *"If you confess with your mouth that Jesus is Lord and believe in your heart that God raised him from the dead, you will be saved. For it is by believing in your heart that you are made right with God, and it is by confessing with your mouth that you are saved."*

> 1 John 1:9 (NIV) — *"If we confess our sins, He is faithful and righteous to forgive us our sins and to cleanse us from all unrighteousness."*

> Acts 16:30-31 (NLT) — *"Then he brought them out and asked, 'Sirs, what must I do to be saved?' They replied, 'Believe in the Lord Jesus and you will be saved, along with everyone in your household.'"*

1 Corinthians 1:30 (NLT) – *"God has united you with Christ Jesus. For our benefit God made him to be wisdom itself. Christ made us right with God; he made us pure and holy, and he freed us from sin."*

These scriptures describe what took place when you invited Jesus into your heart. You were saved (which means you were rescued out of the realm of darkness and brought into the Kingdom of Light, which is God's Kingdom), made right with God, and forgiven of all sin. How amazing is that?!

NEW CREATION

As new creations in Christ, we must now manage our righteousness, not our sin. Righteousness simply refers to our rightness with God and freedom from guilt and sin.

2 Corinthians 5:17 (NLT) – *"This means that anyone who belongs to Christ has become a new person. The old life is gone; a new life has begun!"*

Who lives in us now? What has Jesus given us? (Galatians 2:20)

_____

What nature do we have now? (Colossians 3:9-10)

_____

FULLY FORGIVEN

Romans 6:23 says, *"The wages of sin is death BUT the free gift of God is eternal life through Jesus."* Not only are we forgiven of our sins, but we are also set free from its wages: death. Sin cannot find any expression in a corpse. Our sin nature is dead, so we are acting like a dead person if we sin.

What is necessary for the forgiveness of sins? (Hebrews 9:22)

_____

What did Jesus shedding his blood do for us? (Romans 5:8-10)

_____

What are some things established for us through Jesus' death on the cross?

1 Peter 2:24

_____

2 Corinthians 5:21

_____

Colossians 1:18-22

_____

Colossians 2:13-14

_____

Based on the scriptures above, are all of our sins forgiven (past/present/future)?

_____

In moving forward in your relationship with Christ, you will discover how God created you to reign (have victory) in every area of life. You can live in peace, joy, healing, freedom, prosperity, and more. So, let's dive into more of the amazing things Jesus has done.

FAITH AND GRACE

> Romans 5:17 (NIV) – *"For the sin of this one man, Adam, caused death to rule over many. But even greater is God's wonderful grace and his gift of righteousness, for all who receive it will live in triumph over sin and death through this one man, Jesus Christ."*

When we RECEIVE God's grace, we will reign in life.

> Ephesians 2:8-9 (NASB) – *"For by grace you have been saved through faith; and that not of yourselves, it is the gift of God; not as a result of works, so that no one may boast."*

> Titus 2:11 (NLT) – *"For the grace of God has been revealed, bringing salvation to all people."*

Grace is what God does. Faith is what we do—yet even faith is a gift from God. Grace is something that was established before we ever existed. It has nothing to do with what we do or don't do. By definition, it is "unmerited, unearned, undeserved favor." It is *not* based on our performance;

it is based on the *finished* work (cross & resurrection) of Jesus. By grace, God found us in Jesus before He lost us in Adam. We were associated in Jesus before the fall of the world (Ephesians 1:4), meaning our origin isn't in Adam; it's in Jesus. Through the finished work of Jesus, we have been handed a receipt, not an invoice. No wonder Jesus' message is called the Good News!

Grace doesn't give us a license to sin. It gives us a license to win against sin. Grace enables what it commands. We have been empowered to be victorious in every area of life.

☑ ACTIVATION: GRACE

Take a moment and declare over yourself, "I receive God's grace. Like a sponge, I just soak it all in!" Imagine God pouring water over you. Envision His grace empowering you to live in freedom and victory.

BAPTISM · WATER AND SPIRIT

Acts 2:38 (NLT) – *Peter replied, "Each of you must repent (change the way you think) of your sins and turn to God, and be baptized in the name of Jesus Christ for the forgiveness of your sins. Then you will receive the gift of the Holy Spirit."*

Matthew 28:19 (NLT) – *"Therefore, go and make disciples of all the nations, baptizing them in the name of the Father and the Son and the Holy Spirit."*

There are two kinds of baptism: water and Holy Spirit. Let us consider them separately.

WATER BAPTISM

Being baptized in water is comparable to a burial. For a burial to take place, we must first die. What must we die to before we can be baptized? (Romans 6:1-3)

_____

_____

Paul also correlates water baptism to circumcision – not done with human hands, but a spiritual circumcision done by Christ (Colossians 2:11-12). What is "cut off" during this spiritual circumcision?

Water baptism is a public demonstration of our decision to follow Jesus. Our old nature is dead, and we begin to walk in our new nature in Christ. Invite your friends to come share in your water baptism. It is a great opportunity for them to see and hear what has happened in your life.

Have you been baptized in water? If not, do you want to be baptized right now?

_____

SPIRIT BAPTISM

Jesus wants to empower us with the Holy Spirit. This is called, "baptism in the Holy Spirit."

Matthew 3:11 (NLT) – *"I baptize with water those who repent (change the way they think) of their sins and turn to God. But someone (Jesus) is coming soon who is far greater than I am...He will baptize you with the Holy Spirit and with fire."*

What gift did the Father promise? (Acts 1:4-5)

_____

What did Jesus say his followers would receive when the Holy Spirit came upon them? (Acts 1:8)

_____

What happened to the people when they were filled with the Holy Spirit? (Acts 2:1-4)

_____

Who is this for? (Acts 2:17-18)

_____

We already have the Holy Spirit inside of us (1 Corinthians 3:16). So did over one hundred Christians in John 20:22, who later had the Holy Spirit come upon them (Acts 2:3-4).

ACTIVATIONS

Here are a few practical activations that can help you experience the baptism in the Holy Spirit, hear God, and share your story with others.

☑ ACTIVATION: SPIRIT BAPTISM

Receiving this baptism starts by simply agreeing that you already have the Holy Spirit inside of you (1 Corinthians 3:16). In Acts 2, when the 120 believers were worshipping out loud, they had already received the Holy Spirit INSIDE (John 20:22), and then the Holy Spirit came UPON them in Acts 2.

Just begin to worship Jesus by singing out loud and receive BY FAITH your baptism in the Holy Spirit. You may start to hear words coming out that are not your common language. This is called praying in tongues. Speak out what you are hearing; you're being baptized in the Holy Spirit.

☑ ACTIVATION: HEARING GOD

Who can hear the voice of God? (John 10:14, 27)

_____

Declare over yourself, "I can hear God's voice" and "I have ears to hear Him."

With a partner, simply ask Holy Spirit for a picture or a word (about their destiny or what is happening in their life that you couldn't know on your own) for the other person. Then, share whatever you immediately see or hear. Ask Him what He thinks about you and share what you hear and/or see.

☑ ACTIVATION: SHARE YOUR FAITH

You now have a powerful story. Jesus has completely forgiven you, made you into a new creation, and immersed you in His love. So many others need to hear about the good news of Jesus! Sharing your story with others can bring them into the same encounter you've experienced. Call together some of your friends and, maybe over coffee or dinner, tell them what happened. As you read the Bible, invite your friends to read with you. Your breakthrough and experience can become theirs, too.

READING THE BIBLE

A great place to start reading the Bible is the book of John. Your journey begins with finding out how to become more like Jesus, and John was the closest disciple to Jesus. If something doesn't make sense as you read, stop and ask Holy Spirit to reveal to you what it means (remember, you CAN hear Him). What other book allows you to interact with the author (Holy Spirit) while you read? The Holy Spirit is our teacher. Also, when you meet up with another Christian, ask questions and talk through what you're reading. All of us are on a continual journey of learning. The entire Bible is all about Jesus, and Jesus is all about us. The more we learn about Jesus, the more we learn about ourselves.

PHASE II – YOUR ACCESS & ROLE IN THE KINGDOM

You've made it through Phase I. You've seen that in Jesus you've been made into a new creation, fully forgiven and deeply loved. Congratulations! Now that you've tasted some good morsels, let's dig into more of the meal. As in Phase I, you'll discover more of what God has said in the Bible and understand what it all means for you today. Let's take a look at how God made us and unpack each facet.

SPIRIT, SOUL, AND BODY

> 1 Thessalonians 5:23 (NLT) – *"Now may the peace of God make you holy in every way, and may your whole SPIRIT and SOUL and BODY be kept blameless until our Lord Jesus Christ comes again."*

This verse explains that we have three parts: spirit, soul, and body. Each part is different, so let's examine each of them.

SPIRIT

God is spirit (John 4:24), so He communicates to our born again spirit (our spirit becomes born again through Jesus), through which we also connect with Him. God is anchored in the spiritual world (Kingdom of Heaven) where *all things are possible*. He calls us to live from the reality of Heaven and not to be led and anchored simply in the physical world. We can live from heaven since we are there too! (Ephesians 2:6)

Our spirit is the innermost part of our being. Although it's the center of who we are, it cannot be felt or seen. Everything flows from our spirit, the place where God dwells, speaks, and flows.

What did God put into man at creation? (Genesis 2:7)

_____

The Hebrew word (the Old Testament was written in Hebrew) for *breath* is translated as "spirit." Adam's body and soul (physical, mental, and emotional parts) had no life in them until God's *spirit* was imparted.

Prior to this, we learned about how we were made new (born again). All of that happened in our spirit. Take a few moments and read these scriptures, which tell of the other incredible things that God has deposited in our spirit.

- We have received God's fullness (John 1:16)

- We are holy and without fault in the Father's eyes in Christ (Ephesians 1:4)

- We have a new nature created to be like God, holy and righteous (Ephesians 4:24)

- We are given a new nature (operating system) (Romans 6)

- We are sealed and given the Holy Spirit (Ephesians 1:13)

- We have the measure of faith (Romans 12:3)

As you can see, so much has been given to us because of the finished work of Christ (death, burial and resurrection). Let's unpack a few more scriptures to gain more insight into all that has happened in our spirit.

How close are we to Jesus in our spirit? Is He ever far away? (1 Corinthians 6:17)

_____

Of what does Holy Spirit remind us in our spirit? (Romans 8:16)

_____

What happens when we pray in the Spirit (tongues)? (1 Corinthians 14:14)

_____

When we pray in the Spirit, our spirit prays (with the mind of Christ) in perfect union with Holy Spirit (Romans 8:26-27). What an amazing reality, that we can pray in perfect union with Holy Spirit!

What is produced in us when we renew our mind to agree with what God has placed in our spirit? (Romans 8:6) How do you feel having more peace would change your life?

_____

_____

Our spirit is one with Jesus (1 Corinthians 6:17), which means we are always united. This happened when we asked Jesus into our life. We were baptized into His body (Romans 6:3). This union is what gives us complete access to the Father, Holy Spirit, and the Kingdom of God. The pin code to the Kingdom is IN CHRIST. We have also been united with all believers (1 Corinthians 12:13). How amazing that we are one body with millions of believers across the world because we are one with Jesus!

Our spirit is the real us! *"For as the body without the spirit is dead, so also faith without works is dead"* (James 2:26 NASB). It is where our new nature has been deposited. We must learn to live from this place so we can reign in every area of life.

SOUL

The soul is comprised of our mind, will, and emotions. It is the center of our thoughts, attitudes, and agreements. Just as we can feel in our body, we can also feel in our soul. For example, if someone speaks negatively of us, it hurts our feelings. Though the harm is not physical, it is still felt.

What happens to the human soul (mind, will, and emotions) at death? (1 Corinthians 13:9-12)

_____

What is our responsibility with our soul? (Romans 12:2)

_____

Here, the word *conformed* means "poured into the mold of." In life, we encounter pressures from the world, the devil, and circumstances. Although we can't avoid being melted, we can choose which mold we will be poured into.

The word *transformed* here is the same Greek word (the New Testament was written in Greek) from which we derive "metamorphosis." As we repent/renew our mind (change the way we think by agreeing with what God says and who He is), we come away from being bitter, hurtful, sick, and defeated, and we change into the loving, healed, joyful, victorious person God created us to be. Whatever we think in our soul, our body will go along with for the ride. When our mind is renewed to align with God's truth, it is because we have accepted that God has all the best thoughts, and we want them too. Our lives are transforming to the degree our minds are renewing. The soul is not evil; it's good, and God has redeemed it. It's just not supposed to be in the driver's seat. We are to be led by our spirit, where Holy Spirit dwells.

Have you seen the effects of negative thinking in your life? What have they looked like?

_____

What happens when we are led by our soul? (Romans 8:6)

_____

What else can happen if we are led by our soul? (Ephesians 4:18)

_____

Do we have more than one mind? (James 1:5-8)

_____

What are the results of being double-minded? (James 1:5-8)

_____

Whose mind do we now have in Christ? (1 Corinthians 2:10-16)

_____

What does having His mind give us access to? (1 Corinthians 2:10)

_____

How much truth can we know because of His mind? (1 John 2:20 NKJV)

_____

The Greek word for "all" in the verse above means "to the exclusion of nothing." How amazing is that! We have been given the mind of Christ in our spirit.

We have two minds: our natural mind (our soul) and our spiritual mind (mind of Christ). As we change the way we think (repent) by agreeing with God's truth (His words), we become single-minded. If we don't change the way we think, our two minds come out of alignment, and we are unable to receive anything from God and are unstable in every way (James 1:5-8). A key to the Christian life is training our physical mind to agree with our spiritual mind. We have one nature, but two minds. This isn't simply about positive thinking; it's about aligning our thoughts to God's words. The brain attaches faith to whatever it thinks is true. Every thought is a seed, and our mind is a garden. What thoughts are we letting in? These thoughts are anchored either in truth or in lies. A harvest will be produced through our behavior since all actions are manifested thoughts. We cannot afford to be entertaining thoughts that aren't in God's mind.

BODY

What happens to the human body at death? (1 Corinthians 15:42-44)

Our body doesn't really control anything. It merely goes along with what's happening in the physical world, simply reacting to what it sees, tastes, hears, smells, and feels unless otherwise influenced by the soul (mind, will, and emotions). While our five physical senses are good, they, like our soul, are not to be in the driver's seat. However, if we allow all that God has given us to flow from our spirit to our soul (renew our minds), our behaviors will then match the righteousness we have been freely given in Christ. Our body (flesh) is weak, but our spirit is willing (Matthew 26:41).

THE SUPERNATURAL: OUR AUTHORITY

God is supernatural. He spoke words, and worlds were created. Not only is He supernatural, but He also partners with us so that we can do what His Son does. In John 20:21, Jesus said to us, *"As the Father sent me, now I send you."* Because of our relationship with Jesus, we too can heal the sick, drive out demons, raise the dead, demonstrate God's Kingdom on earth, and more.

What did Jesus go around doing? (Acts 10:38)

_____

Is what Jesus sent us to do any different? (John 20:21)

_____

What has Jesus sent us to do, and what has He given us to
do it? (Matthew 10:1, Luke 9:1-2)

_____

What signs follow those who believe in Jesus? (Mark 16:17-18)

_____

What works can we do if we believe in Jesus? (John 14:12)

_____

What or whom did Jesus need before performing miracles,
signs, and wonders? (Matthew 3:16-17)

_____

What power is inside of us? (Romans 8:11)

_____

Where does His power work, and what can it accomplish?
(Ephesians 3:20)

_____

How are people convinced that the message of Jesus is true,
and how is the message fully presented? (Romans 15:19)

_____

How does God confirm His good news message?
(Hebrews 2:4)

Let's consider electrical power. What happens when we flip the switch to turn on the light in our home? The light turns on, right? Do we need to call the power company and have them send someone over to turn on the light for us? Of course not, for we have an agreement with the power company: we have complete authority to turn on the lights. The power company generates the electricity and delivers it to our place. We aren't the source of the power, but we have access to it and have the authority to use it.

In the same way, Jesus has given us His power and authority. Through relationship with Him, we have come into agreement that He is God and was raised from the dead. To see the power of God manifested through our lives, we have to use the authority He has given us (flip the switch). He is the source of the power, and that very power is working INSIDE us (Ephesians 3:20). The big difference is that we have been given His power for free (grace).

The Gospels (the books Matthew, Mark, Luke, and John) record many miracles performed by Jesus. Almost 60% of the Gospels is composed of Jesus either healing the sick or casting out demons. If we are going to be like Jesus, these miracles should be normal for us, too. We have been sent to do the same thing. How incredible is that? Because He has given us His power and authority, we can re-present Him to the world.

GIFTS AND FRUITS OF THE HOLY SPIRIT

What are some gifts the Holy Spirit likes to give out?
(1 Corinthians 12:4-11)

What's the highest goal regarding these gifts?
(1 Corinthians 14:1)

What should be propelling us to walk in these gifts?
(1 Corinthians 13:1-3)

What are the fruits that the Holy Spirit will produce in our lives? (Galatians 5:22-23)

Which fruit is the greatest? (1 Corinthians 13:13)

As can be seen, we can witness amazing things with the supernatural power of God. However, if we don't have love, they are meaningless. Love wins all the time. Love is a noun before it's a verb. The Father's love is perfect and drives out all fears and anxieties (1 John 4:18). We must receive His love, love ourselves, and then love others. We can only love others to the degree we love ourselves. Jesus said in Matthew 22:39, *"Love your neighbor as yourself."*

☑ ACTIVATION: SUPERNATURAL HEALING

Isaiah 53:5 says, *"By His stripes we WERE healed."* Roughly two thousand years ago, Jesus established healing for ALL. We have His full authority to command healing into people's bodies. It's a promise upon which we can confidently stand. We can speak with boldness for sickness, pain, and disease to go away in Jesus' name.

Take a Christian friend with you and pray for someone who is sick. If you don't know anyone who is ill, go out and look for someone who visibly needs healing in his or her body (crutches, cast, etc.).

We don't have to beg God to heal. We COMMAND healing into the body. It's not about petitioning God, but proclaiming what has been accomplished already through the finished work of Jesus. His stripes were enough. Therefore, we can pray something like this: "I command healing into your body right now in Jesus' name. Pain, get out now." Or, speak to the condition with a prayer like this: "I speak to your spine to align and command pain to get out now in Jesus' name."

BEING A JESUS FOLLOWER [DISCIPLE]

We've seen how God sent His only begotten Son, Jesus, to Earth and how He healed the sick, drove out demons, etc. Not only did He do those things, but He also partnered with us to do the same and greater works (John 14:12). God isn't using superstars; He loves to use ordinary people to do extraordinary things. Jesus chose twelve regular guys (the people He called disciples) in whom to invest. He wanted them to continue His mission on the earth. Some of Jesus' final words to His disciples are in Matthew 28:18-20, which are called the Great Commission.

Write out the Great Commission in Matthew 28:18-20.

_____

_____

_____

_____

_____

Where does Jesus have complete authority? (Matthew 28:18)

_____

Does Jesus expect us to do this alone? (Matthew 28:20)

_____

What is one skill Jesus said we have when following Him? (Mark 1:17)

_____

When we start following Jesus, what are some things He wants us to do? (Matthew 28:19)

_____

☑ ACTIVATION: FOLLOWING JESUS

What do you think it means to follow Jesus? Write it out.

_____

_____

_____

What did Jesus say He would cause His disciples to become as they followed Him? (Matthew 4:18-20)

_____

What did Jesus tell His disciples to do? (Acts 10:42)

_____

How did Jesus treat sinners (those who haven't believed yet)? (Mark 2:13-17)

_____

How did Jesus respond when His disciples wanted to take vengeance on people who didn't welcome Jesus? (Luke 9:51-56)

_____

What did Jesus say would result from the disciples' lives? (John 15:8)

_____

What is the secret to being very fruitful? (John 15:5)

_____

Where did Jesus say His disciples would be His witnesses when they received power from the Holy Spirit? (Acts 1:8)

_____

What happened as new disciples began to do life together with other disciples? (Acts 2:42-47)

_____

Every follower of Jesus has been commissioned to do what Jesus did and to share the incredible things He has done in us. We all have a story that we can share with others who haven't encountered Jesus yet. We call these people "missed" because God misses them so much. He has created them and longs to be in relationship with them. Your life can be the very encounter with God they need.

We should always be ready to share our powerful story of how Jesus has transformed our lives.

☑ ACTIVATION: MAKING FOLLOWERS OF JESUS (DISCIPLES)

Write out your personal story with Jesus. Focus on a few areas:

- What was life like before you began a relationship with Jesus?

- How did you start a relationship with Jesus?

- What has changed in your life since Jesus has come in?

Now share this with someone or a group of people who don't have a relationship with Jesus. Your friends are the best place to start since they know you. Invite them over and eat some food together. This is a powerful way for others to hear about the transformation Jesus has brought into your life!

SPENDING TIME WITH GOD

God longs to be in friendship with us. Jesus says in John 15:15, "*I no longer call you slaves, because a master doesn't confide in his slaves. Now you are called friends, since I have told you everything the Father told me*" (NLT). God loves to talk with us as we live out life. We can talk to God throughout our day, and we don't have to talk in some religious manner. Just talk to him from your heart. You can ask lots of questions, just like a child would, and our Father will take the time to answer. Let's explore what the Bible says, as well as a few practical ways we can engage with God.

PRAYER

What does the prayer of a righteous person accomplish? (James 5:16)

_____

What's important to do when we pray? (Mark 11:22-25)

_____

What did Jesus tell His disciples prayer would help with? (Matthew 26:40-41)

_____

☑ ACTIVATION: PRAYER

Thanksgiving is an amazing way to communicate with God. Simply thanking Him for what He has done in our lives and all the incredible promises He has given us stirs our hearts toward Him. Our faith abounds in thanksgiving (Colossians 2:7). Thanksgiving isn't simply reserved for crises; it must be a continual flow in our lives. It is an act of our will and an activity that attracts heaven. 1 Thessalonians 5:16-18 says, *"Always be joyful. Never stop praying. Be thankful in all circumstances, for this is God's will for you who belong to Christ Jesus"* (NLT).

Here are a few sample prayers that can help kick-start some conversation with God.

"Thank you, Father, for every provision you've already set aside for every circumstance, relationship, and obstacle I face. You're so good and loving. I choose to receive your love and grace today."

"Thank you, Father, that you love my friends and family even more than I do. Allow me to speak into their lives about how loving you are towards them. I thank you that you desire them to be in relationship with you, and I declare that they will be in Jesus' name."

Again, these are just examples of how we can engage in conversation with God. Thankfulness is always a great way to talk to Him. Now, it's your turn. Talk to Papa God and tell Him about your day and thank Him for all that He has done.

THE BIBLE

Another way we can spend time connecting with God is by reading the Bible. It's the only book where you can read and interact with the author at the same time.

What does God speaking His words and then worlds being created tell you about the words of God?

_____

What do the words of God do? (Hebrews 4:12)

_____

Psalm 119 has a lot to say about God's Word. Take a few moments and read through it and see what sticks out to you.

☑ ACTIVATION: THE BIBLE

As you read through Psalm 119, ask Holy Spirit to open the eyes of your heart (Ephesians 1:17-19). Just simply ask something like this, "Holy Spirit, reveal to me the truths of what I am reading."

Then write down anything you hear or sense:

_____

_____

_____

_____

_____

WORSHIP

Worshipping God is another way we can interact with Him. Worship can include things like singing, painting, playing instruments, dancing, working, etc. (but certainly not limited to these). Everything we do in life can be an act of worship. It's much like letting all the goodness He has poured into us come spilling out. Worshipping God many times is like hitting the refresh button, causing our minds to reboot and speak towards truth.

Here are some examples of worship in the Bible. Read these scriptures and list a few examples of how people worshipped God:

Psalm 30:4

_____

Psalm 33:2-3

_____

Colossians 3:16-17, 23

_____

Psalm 150:1-6

_____

Acts 4:24

_____

How should we worship Jesus? (1 Peter 3:15)

_____

☑ ACTIVATION: WORSHIP

Here are some suggestions to connect with God in worship:

Turn on some worship music (ask a Christian friend for some if you don't have any). As the music plays, speak out loud of all the good things about God and what He has done for you.

Get a canvas, ask God for a picture, and paint what you see.

Remember, worship doesn't have to involve just singing or music. It's about placing our attention and affection on Him. Our soul (mind, will, and emotions) becomes filled with His goodness and love. He is so worthy of our worship!

The last suggestion would be to buy a journal so you can write, draw, and record all that God is going to show you, speak to you, and more.

PHASE III — YOUR IDENTITY & PURPOSE IN JESUS

Great job for making it to Phase III! We hope that you have seen how much the finished work of Jesus (death and resurrection) has done for us. In Phase II, we focused on our access to the supernatural power and authority of Jesus, being a disciple, spending quality time with Him, and the importance of our triune being: spirit, soul, and body.

We are now going to traverse into the goodness of God and the reality of God as a Father. God is so good, and He loves to lavish that goodness onto His kids.

> James 1:17 (NLT) — *"Whatever is GOOD and PERFECT comes down to us from God the Father, who created all the lights in the heavens. He never changes or casts a shifting shadow."*

How does God see us? (Romans 8:16)

_____

_____

Who are we in God the Father, and what does He want us to call Him? (Romans 8:15)

_____

Who did Jesus represent in all that He did and said? (John 5:19-23)

_____

What did God the Father say to Jesus BEFORE He performed any miracles? (Matthew 3:16-17)

_____

After someone comes into relationship with Jesus, describe how his or her relationship with God changes. (Galatians 4:3-7)

_____

EARTHLY FAMILY TEMPLATE

Each of us was brought up differently. For some, childhood was a positive experience, and for others, it was not. These positive and negative memories and experiences can shape even our interpretation of words. For example, if some of our negative experiences were with an earthly father, it can cause some to dislike even the term "father." In contrast, our heavenly Father is perfect in every way, and His love is unconditional. He is not a perfectionist, an abuser, or distant in any way. Father God cannot be properly represented aside from His goodness. He is good!

John 14:18 (NLT) – *"No, I will not abandon you as orphans; I will come to you."*

- Our earthly father meets 3 basic human needs: Identity, Protection, and Provision.

- Our earthly mother meets 3 basic human needs: Nurturing, Comforting, and Teaching.

- Our siblings and/or friends meet 2 basic human needs: Companionship and Communication.

If these "human needs" are not met, it can sometimes lead to an "orphan mindset." This can look like the scenario below:

When needs are expressed but not met, there is a lack of comfort. When we have a lack of comfort, we become afraid. When we are afraid, we want control. The only way to remain in control is to manipulate those around us.

This describes an orphan mindset. Even while in a relationship with God, we can still operate in these destructive patterns (mindsets). Getting free from these patterns (mindsets) starts with encountering the goodness of God.

☑ ACTIVATION: FAMILY TEMPLATE

Our experiences with each of our family members often determine how we see the Godhead (Father, Son, Holy Spirit). Our earthly father correlates with how we see God the Father. Our mother correlates with how we see Holy Spirit. Finally, our siblings/friends correlate with how we see Jesus. Some of our experiences were negative and have possibly given us a wrong view of one or more of the Godhead. Write out what you experienced with each family member according to the basic needs each meets.

FATHER

Identity – Were you encouraged growing up? Did you hear, "I'm proud of you"? Did you have to be perfect?

_____

Protection – Did you feel safe with your dad - physically & emotionally? Did he stand up for you? When you were scared, did he help you feel safe?

_____

Provision – Were your needs provided for? Did your dad get you "extras" in life, or did he just provide for basic needs? Did you grow up in poverty?

_____

MOTHER

Nurturing – How did your mom respond to emotional needs in your life? Did your mom validate your emotions?

_____

Comforting – Did your mom comfort you when you cried? When you hurt yourself, did your mom tell you it was going to be okay?

_____

Teaching – Did your mom help you with homework? Did she help you understand the world around you? Did you have to be perfect?

_____

SIBLINGS (OR FRIENDS IF YOU HAD NO SIBLINGS)

Companionship – Did you have positive or negative interactions with your siblings/friends? What emotions are connected with those memories?

_____

Communication – Did you have a strong emotional connection with your siblings/friends? Were you able to be yourself around them?

_____

WHAT'S GOD LIKE? (FATHER, SON, HOLY SPIRIT)

Does God's love wane at all? (Psalm 107:1)

_____

1 John 4:8 says, "*God is love.*" 1 Corinthians 13 is an entire chunk of scripture that describes the look and feel of "love." Read 1 Corinthians 13:4-7, and then write what stands out to you. As you read, replace the word "love" with "Father." Since God is love, this chapter is describing what He is like.

_____

_____

_____

_____

_____

_____

How much did the Father provide for us? (John 3:16)

_____

Where does Father God get our provision? (Ephesians 1:3)

_____

Where is our safe place in Him? (Colossians 3:3)

_____

What is one of the roles of Holy Spirit in our lives? (John 14:16)

_____

What does Holy Spirit teach us? (John 14:26)

_____

Can we be friends with Jesus? (John 15:15)

_____

Will Jesus ever leave us or forsake us? (Matthew 28:20, Deuteronomy 31:6)

_____

Who can hear God? (John 8:47, 10:27)

_____

☑ ACTIVATION: TRIUNE GODHEAD (FATHER, JESUS, HOLY SPIRIT)

Let's take some time now and identify any lies with which we may have come into agreement that connect with our experiences with our dad, mom, and/or siblings/friends. Just ask Holy Spirit to reveal any lies where there's agreement. For example, perhaps our dad was emotionally distant growing up. Do we see God the Father as distant? If the answer is yes, then speak out loud saying, "I forgive my dad for being emotionally distant." Then, break agreement with the lie that God the Father is distant by saying something like, "I break agreement with the lie that Father God is distant." Finally, declare the truth – in this case, a verse like Hebrews 13:5. Do this for any lie where agreement has been made:

Dad:

Mom:

Siblings/Friends:

WHO DO WE THINK WE ARE: IDENTITY

Identity is the echo of belief. It always precedes actions. We behave according to what we believe to be true, so outward behavior is simply a reflection of the truth we believe. This is why it is crucial that we understand who God is (His nature) and who He is for us. Identity is the foundation of all things. We live *from* our identity in Christ, not towards it. The access code of the Kingdom of God is "IN CHRIST." Our personal security is built upon our understanding of who God is for us (Hebrews 3:6, 14). Assurance allows us to become who we were destined to be.

We live in Christ, not our circumstances (Colossians 3:3). What Jesus is to us, we become to others. We can only reveal what God has made real (our agreement). We cannot realize our true identity outside of the affection of God. Our identity is only in Him. Both heaven and hell are asking us the same question: "Who do you *think* you are?" Our answer to that question affects every area of our lives.

What did man have to do to become like God? (Genesis 1:26-27)

_____

Who told us we had to do something in order to be like God? (Genesis 3:4-5)

_____

Adam and Eve didn't stand firm in the truth of their identity (they were already like God). They chose to agree with the devil (empower him) and forgot who they were (Genesis 3:13). Adam lost his crown in the Garden because he was silent when he should have spoken. When we believe a lie, we empower the liar, the devil. When we believe the Truth (Jesus), we then empower truth, and the truth is what sets us free (John 8:32).

For most of us, there are four points of view regarding our identity:

1. The devil's perspective: the accuser of the brethren

2. Outside views: the way others see us

3. Personal choice: the way we choose to see ourselves

4. The way God sees us

What are the results of coming into agreement with each of these in our identity?

_____

_____

_____

God is the only one who truly knows who we are. Our actions do not equate to our identity or value to God. We are of equal value to Jesus in the Father's eyes.

What is our value to the Father? (1 John 3:1)

_____

Let's examine what else God has to say about who we REALLY are. Read each scripture and then write out what He says about us:

(John 1:12, Galatians 3:26)

(2 Corinthians 5:17)

(Galatians 4:6-7, Romans 8:17)

(2 Corinthians 5:18-19)

(Ephesians 1:1, Colossians 1:2)

(Ephesians 2:20)

(Philippians 3:20)

(1 Corinthians 12:27)

(1 Corinthians 3:16, 6:19)

(John 15:15-16)

(Ephesians 4:24)

_____

(Matthew 5:13-14)

_____

(Colossians 3:4)

_____

(1 Thessalonians 5:5)

_____

(Romans 8:37)

_____

(1 Peter 2:5)

_____

(1 Peter 2:9)

_____

(Ephesians 1:3)

_____

These are some amazing scriptures that give us an idea of what God thinks about us. Why would we choose to believe anything other than what He says about us? A really practical way to renew our minds to our true identity is to speak these and other scriptures out loud throughout our week. It will remind us of the truth, and it is the truth that sets us free.

Job 22:28 says, "*You will also decree a thing and it WILL be established for you*" (NASB). When we decree (speak out loud) what He says about us, it will help us to walk out who we really are in Him. Ecclesiastes 8:4 says, "*His command is backed by power*" (NLT). We are kings in Christ, so our words have power.

The progression of our identity is this: the Holy Spirit reveals Jesus to us, Jesus presents us to the Father, and the Father reveals us to the world. Getting to know each of them is paramount to walking in the fullness of our identity.

SEXUALITY AND GOD

God designed sex. Everything God makes is good. At the same time, we have to take what is good and allow that to flow faithfully through us in the right context. Our sexuality is a normal part of how God made us. He desires to see that part of us fulfilled in the proper place.

Satan has wreaked havoc in this area in many lives. For some of us, we may have experienced the horror of sexual abuse, rape, or even incest. But no matter what hand we have been dealt, God can deal with any hand and turn it into good. He can bring healing to ALL areas of our lives, including our sexuality. Let's take a look at some scriptures and delve into God's perspective on sexuality.

In the beginning, for what kind of relationship did God design sex? (Genesis 2:18-25)

_____

_____

What is God's perspective on marriage between a man and woman? (Hebrews 13:4)

_____

What relationship did God establish for sexual intimacy? (Ephesians 5:31)

_____

What do sex and the union between husband and wife illustrate? (Ephesians 5:32)

_____

The union of a man and woman in marriage is a powerful picture of the relationship between Jesus and the Church. This is why a sexual relationship expressed in the marriage of a man and woman is crucial to God's purposes in our lives and in the world.

Sex is not only a physical act, but also a spiritual act. It was designed for pleasure, procreation, and the expression of a sacred aspect of God's nature. Sex within a life-long commitment between a husband and wife is an amazing manifestation of God's nature.

How should we treat the opposite sex? (1 Timothy 5:1-2)

_____

What happens spiritually when two people have sex? (1 Corinthians 6:12-17)

_____

_____

What happens in our spirit when we are joined with Jesus? (1 Corinthians 6:17)

_____

How should we respond to the temptation of sexual immorality? (1 Corinthians 6:18)

_____

How does God see our body? (1 Corinthians 6:19)

_____

How are we to use our body? (Romans 6:13)

_____

What kind of habitual lifestyle choices prevent people from inheriting the Kingdom of God? (1 Corinthians 6:9-10)

_____

_____

What happens to anyone who was once immersed in any of the lifestyles listed above, but now believe in and follow Jesus? (1 Corinthians 6:11)

_____

How does Jesus treat a woman caught in the act of sex outside the union of marriage (adultery)? How did the religious teachers treat her? (John 8:1-11)

_____

_____

From Jesus' example here, how should we treat others expressing a lifestyle of sexual sin?

_____

☑ ACTIVATION: SEXUALITY AND GOD

For all of us, before believing in and following Jesus, we were trapped in lifestyles that weren't healthy. We saw in Phase 1 that through Jesus we are FULLY forgiven once for all time. No matter what we have done, He paid for all of our sins.

In Matthew 10:8, Jesus says, *"Freely you have received; freely give."* Not only are we forgiven, but we must also give forgiveness away. Though this may sometimes be the hardest part of the journey, it can bring some of the biggest breakthroughs in our lives.

Take a moment and thank Jesus for His forgiveness. Speak out loud how grateful you are for His paying the price for all of your sins. Then ask Holy Spirit if you need to forgive yourself and/or others. Perhaps you had a breach into your sexuality through abuse, rape, incest, etc. Forgiveness is a choice. Initiate the process by speaking out loud something like this:

> *"I choose to forgive (* <u>insert name here</u> *) for what you did. You don't owe me anything, and I choose to bless your life in Jesus' name."*

(Forgiveness doesn't mean we have to trust the person. It is a process that takes time to move from our head to our heart, and that is okay. It's about continuing to choose to forgive.)

Jesus not only forgives us, but He also desires to heal every part of us (physically, emotionally, and spiritually). Invite Jesus to heal any wounds inflicted by others or yourself. You can simply pray something like this:

> *"Jesus, I invite you to heal all my wounds. I have chosen to forgive. Now I ask that You do what only You can do. I receive Your healing touch and thank You that it is by Your stripes I am healed."*

One of the biggest benefits of living a lifestyle of forgiveness is that it closes the door to the devil. When we have unforgiveness in our hearts, it allows the devil to afflict our bodies and/or torment our minds. When we choose to forgive, the devil has no access.

SPIRITUAL FAMILY

The Kingdom of God is a family affair. We are all His children who have been adopted through Jesus, and He is very happy about it (Ephesians 1:5). There is something very powerful that occurs when we gather together as Jesus' disciples to encourage each other, celebrate, laugh, learn, etc.

> Acts 2:42 (NLT) – *"All the believers devoted themselves to the apostles' teaching and to fellowship, and to sharing in meals, and to prayer."*

All over the world, disciples of Jesus gather to worship, love each other, become equipped as world changers, and more. This is often called "church." In the New Testament, when referring to church, Jesus used the Greek word "*ekklesia.*" It literally means, "called out." We are called out of darkness to demonstrate the power, love, and authority of Jesus on the earth. The church is a living organism, not a static institution.

There are many different expressions of church in all sorts of cultures, but the styles and models of church are not what are important. What should be the focus is gathering around the presence of God, loving each other, standing on His truth, and listening to and obeying Him in order to bring His light to the campuses, cities, and nations. Now, let's dive into the Bible to see what it says about disciples gathering together.

Who builds the church? (Matthew 16:18)

_____

What did the first disciples do when they came together? (Acts 2:42)

_____

What did normal life look like for the first disciples as they gathered together? (Acts 2:42-47)

_____

_____

_____

What does Paul call the people of God as they follow Jesus together? (1 Corinthians 12:27)

_____

We are called to re-present Jesus to the earth. When we do this together and our love for one another is genuine, it has a great impact. Jesus said in John 13:35, "*Your love for one another will prove to the world that you are my disciples.*"

Together we are Jesus' body. What an amazing picture of spiritual family! We all have a vital part to play, and no one part is more important than the other. Let's take a closer look into what this means for us.

What are some different parts of the Body of Christ? (1 Corinthians 12:28)

_____

_____

What does Paul say about the importance of each part of the Body of Christ? (1 Corinthians 12:14-20)

_____

_____

What does he say about those who think they can go solo? (1 Corinthians 12:21)

_____

How should different parts of the Body treat each other? (1 Corinthians 12:25-26)

_____

What are some core leadership roles God has given as gifts to the church? (Ephesians 4:11)

_____

_____

Why did God give these leadership gifts? (Ephesians 4:12-13)

_____

How is the Body of Christ connected and held together? (Ephesians 4:16)

_____

How should we treat spiritual leaders who help us grow in our faith in Jesus? (Hebrews 13:7, 13:17)

_____

_____

What does being a leader look like in Jesus' perspective? (Luke 22:24-27, John 13:1-17)

_____

_____

As we can see, gathering together is vital to our growth and seeing His Kingdom flow through our lives and into the world. We need each other! It is important to be in a local expression of Jesus' body (a spiritual family), and the amazing part is that we are connected to the global family of God, too.

What does a healthy spiritual family look like? Here are some signs of a healthy (not perfect) spiritual family:

- Loving one another (John 13:34-35)

- Devoted to and honoring one another (Romans 12:10)

- Encouraging one another (Romans 14:19)

- Accepting one another (Romans 15:7)

- Forgiving one another (Ephesians 4:32)

- Teaching one another (Colossians 3:16)

- Living in peace with each other (1 Thessalonians 5:13)

- Offering hospitality to one another (1 Peter 4:9)

- Confessing sins to one another (James 5:16)

Let's now take a look at some examples of how and where new churches grew in the Bible.

Where did the first disciples gather? (Acts 2:46)

_____

Where did Peter go to bring the Good News (message of Jesus) to Cornelius, his family, and his friends? (Acts 10:24-29)

_____

What happened as a result? (Acts 10:44-48)

_____

What we can see from these examples is that church is the family of God. The church isn't so much about a building or a location, although there is nothing wrong with buildings. The gathering place isn't the most important thing. Gathering around His presence, loving each other, and loving the world are the most vital elements of the church.

You can bring the Kingdom of God to your friends. One way you can do this is by going to their house, loving on them, and sharing and showing the goodness of Jesus. This can be very simple. Focus on a simple vision during your time together: UP (loving Jesus), IN (loving each other), and OUT (loving those missed by God).

Here are some ideas in relation to the simple vision above:

UP

- Spend some time reading and interacting with the Bible. Start in a book like John.

- Read a story in the Bible about Jesus together, ask questions, and dialogue about the story.

- Play some worship music and invite people to ask Holy Spirit to reveal Himself.

- Speak out loud things that Jesus has done that you are thankful for.

In

- Ask Holy Spirit for a word/picture of encouragement for someone.

- Eat a meal together and speak life into each other.

- Read scriptures in the Bible about what it means to love one another.

- Take communion (remembering what Jesus has done; Luke 22:19-20) together with some bread or crackers and some juice.

OUT

- Go theocaching—ask Holy Spirit for clues for those who need encouragement/healing/etc. in your community. Then go out and find them.

- Invite some of your friends who aren't Christian to read the Bible together over a meal.

- Go out and find people who need healing in their bodies and pray for them.

- Eat out at a local restaurant and call the owners out to let them know you are going to be declaring favor and prosperity on their business.

Congratulations on making it through all three phases! This is only the beginning in your journey with Jesus. So many life-changing things are ahead for you. This tool was all about helping you to jumpstart your relationship with Jesus by discovering all that He has done. We cannot continue to grow in isolation, so staying connected with Christians and involved in a spiritual family will be crucial to your continued growth and impact on the world. There is so much more to learn and experience in Jesus! Thanks so much for taking the time to walk through this.

Receive this declaration over your life today:

Because you're in Christ, you will grow in favor with God and man. You have been fully forgiven and have been co-included, co-crucified, co-raised and are now co-seated with Jesus. Jesus has commissioned you to heal the sick, raise the dead, drive out demons, and make followers of Jesus. Because you have the mind of Christ, you have access to the wisdom of God. You are the light of the world and the salt of the earth in Christ. Your identity is secure in Jesus because you originated in Him. All the blessings of heaven are attracted to you as you walk in your inheritance in Christ. You live in the abundance of the Kingdom of God and have more than enough for your life and for all those that God brings into your life.

All praise, honor, and glory to Jesus!

Made in the USA
Charleston, SC
05 September 2013